T

EXPLORING THE HUMAN BODY

The Skeleton and Muscles

Carol Ballard

FRANKLIN WATTS
LONDON•SYDNEY

First published in 2005 by
Franklin Watts
96 Leonard Street
London EC2A 4XD

Franklin Watts Australia
Level 17/207 Kent Street
Sydney NSW 2000

Produced by Arcturus Publishing Ltd,
26/27 Bickels Yard, 151–153 Bermondsey Street, London SE1 3HA

The right of Carol Ballard to be identified as the author of this work has been
asserted by her in accordance with the Copyright, Designs and Patents Act
1988.

Series concept: Alex Woolf
Editor: Alex Woolf
Designer: Peta Morey
Artwork: Michael Courtney
Picture researcher: Glass Onion Pictures
Consultant: Dr Kristina Routh

Picture Credits
Science Photo Library: 5 (Tony McConnell), 7 (Department of Clinical Radiology,
Salisbury District Hospital), 9 (CNRI), 11 (Hattie Young), 13 (D. Roberts),
15 (Oscar Burriel), 17 (Zephyr), 23 (BSIP / Chassenet), 25 (Coneyl Jay),
27 (BSIP, Barrelle), 28 (Sheila Terry).
Topfoto: 18, 20, 29 (David Wimsett / UPPA).

Every attempt has been made to clear copyright. Should there be any
inadvertent omission, please apply to the publisher for rectification.

A CIP catalogue record for this book is available from the British Library

ISBN 0 7496 5966 1

Printed in Singapore

Contents

What are Skeletons and Muscles?

This picture shows how your bones and muscles are arranged inside your body.

Your skeleton of bones provides a framework that supports the rest of your body. It protects important organs, allows you to move, and gives your body its shape.

There are two hundred and six bones in your skeleton. Some of these are made up from smaller bones joined together. Each bone is exactly the right shape, size and strength for the job it has to do. For example, your thigh bones are long and straight, giving your legs their shape. They are also very strong, to carry the weight of your body.

Your skeleton has several main parts. The bones of your head and face make up your skull. A bony column called your spine runs down the centre of your back. Your chest is made from the bones of your ribcage. Your arms and hands are hung from a bony crossbar called the pectoral girdle, and your legs and feet are hung from a ring of bone called the pelvic girdle.

The places where two or more bones meet are called joints. Knees, ankles, elbows and wrists are all

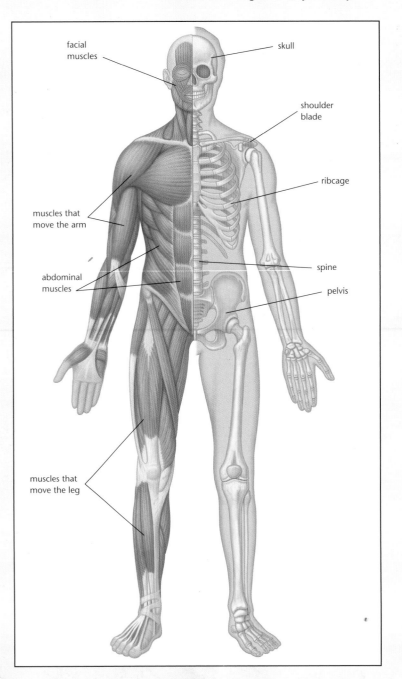

facial muscles

skull

shoulder blade

muscles that move the arm

ribcage

abdominal muscles

spine

pelvis

muscles that move the leg

joints. Tough fibres called ligaments hold the bones together at each joint. They also allow the bones to move past each other, so that you can bend and move parts of your body.

Bones cannot move by themselves. They have to be pulled into new positions by stretchy bands called muscles. Some muscles, such as those that move your thigh bones, are powerful and allow large movements. Other muscles are tiny, such as those that control the movements of your eyeballs. As well as moving your bones, muscles also help you to keep your balance and to stay upright.

You can see the shapes of this man's muscles under his skin.

Not all muscles are attached to bones. Some, like those around your mouth, are attached to skin. Others carry out important jobs inside your body, such as helping food to pass along your digestive system, and allowing you to breathe. Your heart is the most important muscle in your body – it pumps blood around your body every minute of every day, whether you are awake or asleep.

Case notes

What would I be like without a skeleton?

Your skeleton gives your body its shape – without it, you would just be a shapeless jelly-like blob! You would not be able to move around, as there would be no bones for the muscles to pull. You would not be able to pick anything up, kick a ball, ride a bicycle – in fact, you wouldn't really be able to do anything at all!

Inside a Bone

We might think of bones as solid objects, but they are not as simple as that. They are made up from several different layers, complete with a blood supply and nerves. They are specially designed to be strong and light.

Most bones have a tough outer layer that contains nerves and blood vessels. Inside this is a strong, hard layer made of a material called compact bone. Blood vessels and nerves run through holes in the compact bone to the inner layer, called spongy bone. Spongy bone is a mesh of bone pieces. A soft jelly called bone marrow fills the spaces between them. Red bone marrow, found at the ends of bones, helps to produce red blood cells. Yellow bone marrow, found in the middle areas of bones, is mainly fat.

This diagram shows the layers inside a bone.

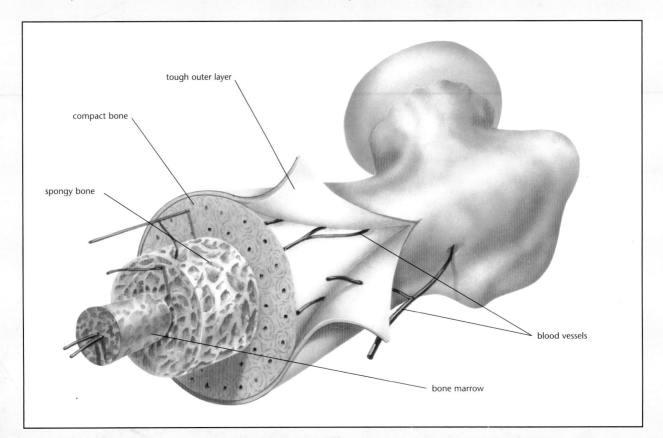

tough outer layer

compact bone

spongy bone

blood vessels

bone marrow

This X-ray shows broken bones in the lower arm.

Bones are living tissues, just like the rest of your body. The blood vessels running through the bones bring oxygen and nutrients for the bones to use. They also carry away waste chemicals that the bones produce. Bones need to communicate with the brain. The nerves in the bones carry information to the brain about bone pain or damage.

Nearly three quarters of bone material is made up of minerals such as calcium, phosphorus, magnesium and zinc. These minerals make the bone rigid. In young children, the bones are slightly soft and flexible but they become stronger and more rigid as more minerals are deposited. Bones retain their full strength for most of an adult's life. In older people, though, some minerals may be lost from bones, making them weaker and more brittle.

Bones act as a mineral store for the body. If your body has plenty of calcium, your bones will store any that is not needed. If there is too little calcium, your bones will release some for use by other parts of your body.

Case notes

What happens when a bone gets broken?

Just as your body is able to grow new skin to heal a cut, so it can grow new bone to mend a broken bone. Doctors make sure that the two parts of the bone are in a straight line and then wrap them in plaster to stop them moving. Slowly, new bone forms at the broken ends and the bone joins back together. This may take a few weeks or even months if a large bone is badly broken.

Bone Shapes

Bones come in a variety of different shapes and sizes, depending on their position in the body and the job they have to do. There are five main bone shapes:

- **Long bones** are long and nearly straight. The bones in your arms and legs are long bones. They are strong and are good at acting as levers. These bones play an important part in moving your body.
- **Short bones** are small bones and are roughly cube shaped. The bones in your wrists and ankles are short bones. They can slide easily past each other, so that these joints are flexible.
- **Flat bones** are thin, curved bones. The ribs, breastbone, shoulder blade and some skull bones are all flat bones. Their shape makes them strong so they can provide good protection for other parts of your body. For example, your skull protects your brain, and your ribs and breastbone protect your heart and lungs.
- **Irregular bones** come in all sorts of strange shapes. The bones of your face and spine are all irregular bones.

This picture shows where different types of bone are found in the human body.

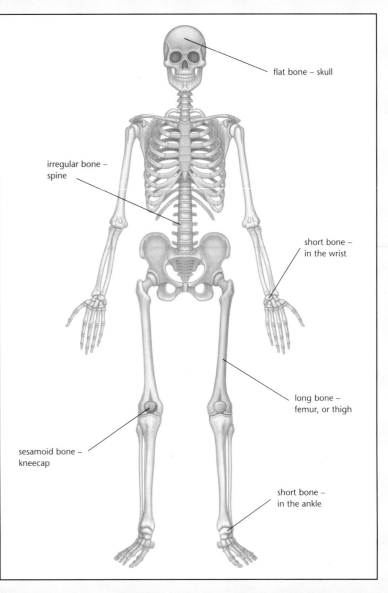

flat bone – skull

irregular bone – spine

short bone – in the wrist

long bone – femur, or thigh

sesamoid bone – kneecap

short bone – in the ankle

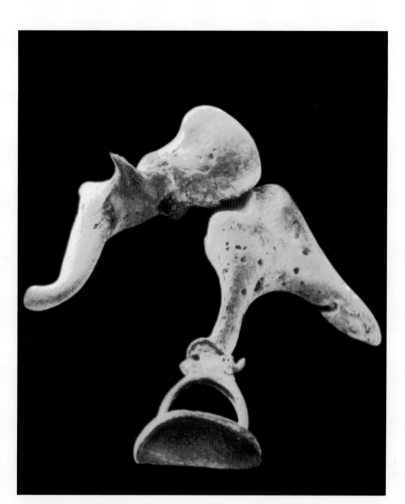

These tiny, irregular bones link together inside your ear to carry sound vibrations.

- **Sesamoid bones** get their name from sesame seeds, which are the same shape (but very much smaller). They are found at joints and help to make the joint work smoothly. The kneecap is a sesamoid bone.

People do not all have exactly the same number of bones. When a baby is born, it may have three hundred bones. During childhood, many join together, making the two hundred and six bones of most adult skeletons. Some bones may not fuse completely, and so small extra bones are left. These are called accessory bones and are most often found in a person's feet. A baby's skull bones are separate when it is born and they slowly join together to form the skull. The joins between these bones are called sutures. Small accessory bones, known as sutural bones, may be found between the joins.

Case notes

How do bones grow?

As we grow from babies into children and teenagers, we all get bigger. This means that, along with the rest of our bodies, our bones have to grow. At each end of a bone is a special area called a growth plate. This makes new bone material on its inside edge, so the bone slowly gets longer. The growth plate stops making new bone material when you have reached your full adult size.

Joints

A joint is a place where two or more bones meet. Here, the bones can move easily past each other, allowing you to move parts of your body.

Most joints are covered by a ligament layer called a capsule. Inside this is a thin layer called a synovial membrane. This makes a special fluid that helps to lubricate the joint, so that the bones can move easily. The end of each bone is covered with a protective layer of cartilage, a stiff, rubbery material. The bones are held firmly in place by strong bands of ligaments. These allow the bones to move, but stop them slipping too far apart.

Hinge joints

Elbows and knees are examples of hinge joints. They get their name because they work like a simple hinge, allowing movement in one direction only. To see how these work, hold your arm straight out in front of you with your palm turned upwards. Imagine your lower arm is a door and your upper arm is the fixed doorframe. If you keep your upper arm absolutely still, you can only move your lower arm backwards and forwards, just like a door opening and closing. You cannot turn it from side to side or round in a circle.

Each picture shows a different type of joint.

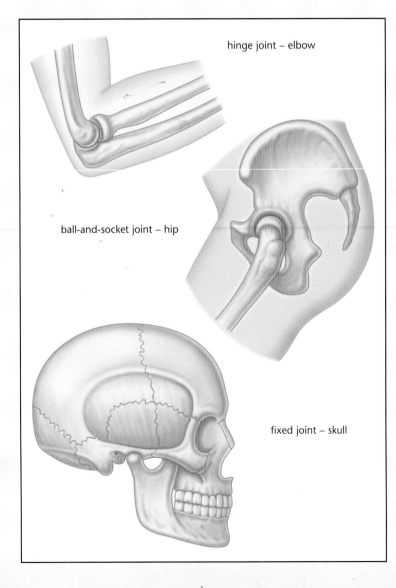

hinge joint – elbow

ball-and-socket joint – hip

fixed joint – skull

Ball-and-socket joints

Shoulders and hips are examples of ball-and-socket joints. These large, strong joints allow much more movement than hinge joints. The joints get their name from the shapes of the bones. One bone has a round, ball-shaped end. This fits snugly into a cup shape at the end of the other bone. In the hip, the ball-shaped top of the thigh bone fits into a cup in the pelvic girdle. The ball can rotate inside the cup, allowing you to move your thigh up and down, backwards and forwards and from side to side.

A nurse is winding a bandage around a sprained ankle. The injury may be painful but it will soon heal.

There are other types of joint too:

- fixed joints, such as those between skull bones, allow no movement
- saddle joints, like the joint between the thumb and wrist, where the bones fit together like a rider on a saddle to allow movement in all directions
- gliding joints, like those in the ankle, allow bones to slide over each other
- condyloid joints, like the knuckles, allow movement up and down as well as side to side
- pivot joints, like that at the base of the skull, allow bones to rotate.

Case notes

What is a sprain?

A sprain is an injury to a joint that occurs when the joint is stretched or twisted too far and the ligaments get damaged. If a joint is sprained, it feels very sore and may be swollen. A sprained wrist is often so sore that the hand movement is limited. A sprained ankle is often too sore to stand on. Sprained joints need to be rested, and an ice pack may help to reduce swelling. Most sprains get better within a few days, although a bad sprain may take much longer.

Face and Head

There are two main parts to your skull. These are the cranium, which is the round part of your skull, and your face, which forms the front part of your skull. Although we usually think of the skull as being one piece of bone, it is actually made up from twenty-two bones. There are seven other bones in your head as well – three tiny bones inside each ear, and a bone that supports your tongue, helping you to speak and swallow.

Cranium

Your cranium is made up from eight bones, joined together like jigsaw pieces. The joins, called sutures, are held together by strong fibres. One large bone (frontal bone) forms the forehead and the tops of the eye sockets. Two large bones (parietal bones) and two smaller bones (temporal bones) form the sides of the head, and a single large bone (occipital bone) forms the back of the head. A single bone (ethmoid bone) forms the inside of the nose and other internal parts of the head. The whole structure is held together by a single bone (sphenoid bone) that stretches across inside the head from one side to the other.

Here you can see how the bones that make the skull fit together.

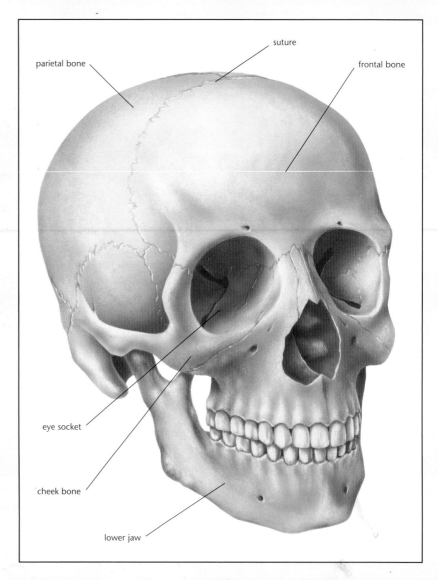

suture

parietal bone

frontal bone

eye socket

cheek bone

lower jaw

This is an X-ray of a human skull. The white areas are bone and the dark areas are spaces.

Face

Your face is made up from fourteen bones. Thirteen are joined together and cannot move. Together they form the lower part of your eye sockets, the ridge of your cheeks and your upper jaw. The other bone is your lower jaw bone (mandible), which is linked to the fixed face bones by a hinge joint at each side. This allows you to move your lower jaw up and down so that you can talk and chew. The bones of the face are not all solid. Some have hollow spaces inside them, called sinuses. These are filled with air and have a thin lining that produces a fluid called mucus. Sinuses are important when you talk and sing, because they help to make your voice sound louder. If you have a bad cold or an infection, the sinuses may become blocked. This is called sinusitis and it can cause an uncomfortable headache.

Case notes

Why isn't there a nose bone on the skull?

If you look at a picture of a human skull you will see that there is a hole where the nose should be. This is because most of the nose has no bone. Two small bones between the eyes form the bridge of the nose. The main part of the nose is stiffened with a piece of cartilage instead of bone.

Back

Your backbone, or spine, runs from the base of your skull down the centre of your back, providing an upright support for the rest of your body. It is made up from a column of thirty-three separate bones stacked one on top of the other. Discs of cartilage in between the bones cushion and protect them so they can move without rubbing together. Each bone is called a vertebra and another name for the spine is the vertebral column. The vertebrae and cartilage discs fit together and are held in place by muscles, tendons and ligaments.

The vertebrae can be thought of in groups. The top seven vertebrae make up the neck and are called cervical vertebrae. Below these are the twelve thoracic vertebrae that make up the back of the chest. Then come five strong lumbar vertebrae that support the powerful back muscles. The five sacral vertebrae below these are separate bones in children, but they slowly fuse together to make one bone called the sacrum. Right at the bottom of the spine is the coccyx, a tiny tail bone made from the fusing together of the last four vertebrae.

Your spine is not absolutely straight. It is slightly curved into an "S" shape. This curve helps to keep your body weight evenly balanced and it also helps to make the spine stronger. The structure of the spine means it is flexible, allowing you to bend backwards and forwards, up and down, from side to side and even to twist around.

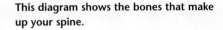

This diagram shows the bones that make up your spine.

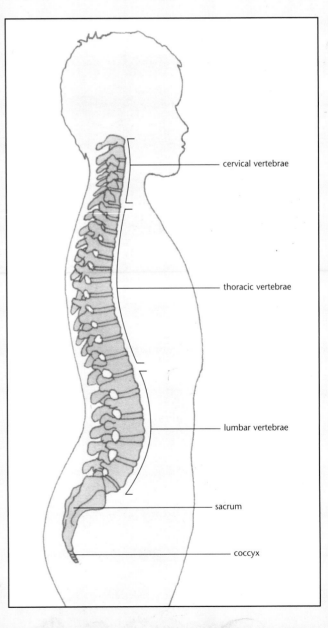

cervical vertebrae

thoracic vertebrae

lumbar vertebrae

sacrum

coccyx

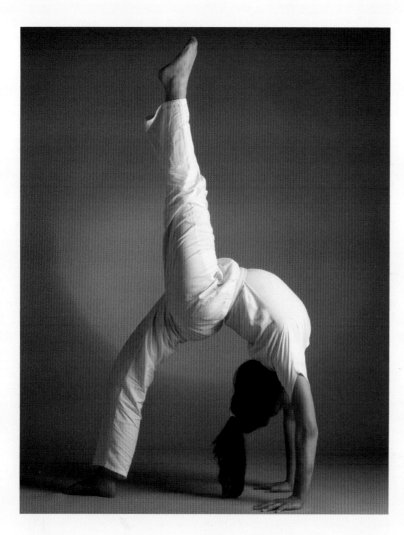

The human spine is strong and flexible, allowing us to bend and stretch in different directions.

Each of the vertebrae is a slightly different shape from the ones above and below it, but they all have the same basic structure. A strong, solid piece of bone, called the body, faces the front of your body. Other pieces of bone, called processes, stick out at the back and sides. Some help the vertebra to stay in place. Others have muscles attached. The body and processes together form a ring of bone.

As the vertebrae are stacked on top of each other, these rings are lined up, with a hollow space running right down the middle of them. This space provides a safe, strong channel for a bundle of nerves called the spinal cord. This runs down the central space, connecting the brain to the rest of the body. If the spinal cord is damaged, the link between the brain and other parts of the body may be broken, resulting in paralysis.

Case notes

What is a slipped disc?

When you stand up normally, the discs between the vertebrae are squashed. Bending awkwardly or lifting heavy objects can cause a disc to become squashed more on one side than on the other. Part of the disc may jut out from between the vertebrae, and can be very painful if the disc presses against the spinal nerves. Resting, gentle exercise and heat treatment often help. In some cases, doctors may operate to remove the damaged disc completely.

Chest

Your chest is made up from a set of twelve pairs of ribs, together with your upper spine at the back and your collarbones and breastbone at the front. These bones are held in place by muscles and pieces of cartilage. Together, this whole structure is called your ribcage.

Your ribcage has two very important jobs to do. First, it provides a strong, bony cage to protect your heart and lungs. Secondly, its flexibility allows you to breathe in and out.

The breastbone, or sternum, is a long, flattish bone that has three parts. The top part has a notch on each side for the ends of the collarbones to fit into. The top pair of ribs are also attached to this part of the sternum. Below this is a longer piece of bone, to which the rest of the ribs are attached. The small, pointed bottom piece of the sternum is made of cartilage in children, but hardens into bone in middle age.

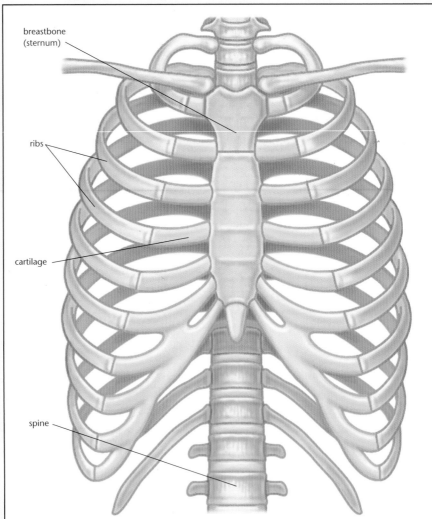

breastbone
(sternum)

ribs

cartilage

spine

The bones of the ribcage showing the attachments to the sternum and spine.

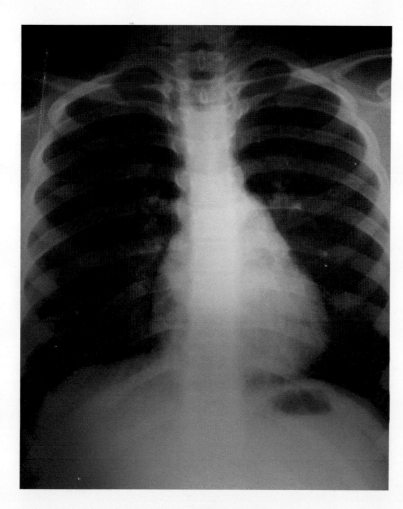

This coloured X-ray shows the shape of the ribcage.

Ribs are curved, flat bones. At the back of the ribcage, each rib is attached to the vertebrae. At the front, the top seven pairs of rib are attached to the sternum by strips of cartilage. The next three pairs are linked together by a single piece of cartilage, which is in turn linked to the sternum. The bottom two pairs of ribs are not linked to the sternum at all and are called floating ribs.

Accidents such as falling heavily or a hard blow to the chest can result in broken ribs. This can be painful but is not usually dangerous, and broken ribs are often left to heal on their own. The chest may be bandaged to prevent further damage. An operation may sometimes be needed, especially if doctors think the broken ribs may damage other parts of the chest such as the heart or lungs.

Case notes

How does my ribcage help me breathe?

When you breathe in, muscles attached to your ribs lift your ribs upwards and outwards. This makes the space inside your chest bigger so that air is sucked into your lungs. When you breathe out, the opposite happens – muscles let your ribs move downwards and inwards so that waste gas is pushed out of your lungs.

Shoulders, Arms and Hands

Your arms hang down from a horizontal bony crossbar called the pectoral girdle. This is made up from your shoulder blades (scapulae) at the back and the collarbones (clavicles) at the front. The shoulder blades are held in place by powerful muscles. Ligaments attach your collarbones to the sternum in the centre of your body and to the shoulder blades at each side.

Your shoulder joints, which link your arms to your shoulder blades, are ball-and-socket joints. These allow your arms to move freely up and down, from side to side, forwards and backwards, and to rotate in a full circle.

Each upper arm has a single long bone called the humerus. The rounded top ends fit into the sockets in the shoulder blades. At the lower end of each humerus is the elbow, a hinge joint that links the upper arm to the lower arm. Your elbows only allow movement in one direction.

Your lower arm has two bones, called the radius and the ulna. These can rotate around each other, allowing you to turn your hands over and back. They are connected to each other by strong fibres.

Your lower arm bones end at your wrist joints. These joints each contain eight small bones. They can slide past each other, so you can move your wrist in any direction.

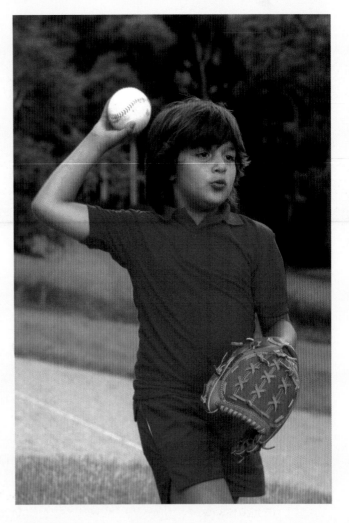

Your shoulder joint allows your arm to swing freely when you throw a ball.

Each hand has an amazing nineteen bones! The flat part of your hand has five long bones, one leading from the wrist to each finger and the thumb. Each finger has three long bones, and the thumbs each have two bones. The joints between the finger bones are hinge joints, allowing you to bend your fingers up and down. The joint at the

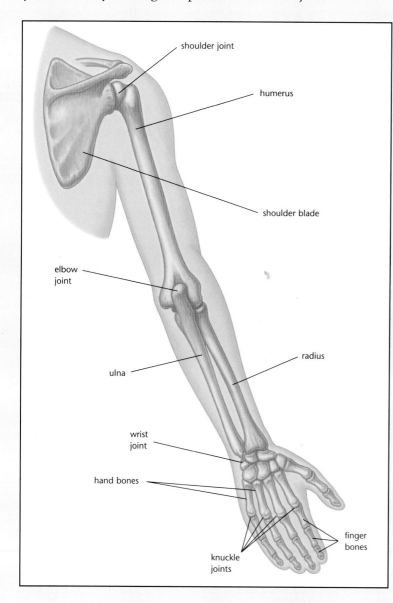

Here you can see how the bones are arranged in your arm and hand.

base of each thumb is a saddle joint, allowing you to rotate your thumb in all directions. This is very special – it means you can pick things up between your finger and thumb, something that only humans and some other primates can do.

Case notes

What is a dislocated shoulder?

This injury is often the result of a sporting accident. The ball at the end of the upper arm bone usually fits snugly into the socket of the shoulder blade, but a very strong twist or other movement can dislodge it. The bones can often be pushed back into their correct positions by a doctor, but the shoulder needs to be rested and kept still afterwards so that the body has a chance to repair any damaged muscles and ligaments.

Hips, Legs and Feet

Your legs hang down from a strong, bony ring called the pelvis. This is made up from your sacrum and coccyx at the back and the hip bones at the front and sides. These bones are held in place by ligaments, and have powerful muscles attached to them.

Your hip joints, linking your legs to your pelvis, are ball-and-socket joints. They allow your legs to move freely up and down, from side to side, forwards and backwards, and to rotate in a full circle. Although the structure of the hip joints is similar to that of the shoulder joints, your legs cannot move quite as freely as your arms. This is because the strong ligaments that hold each hip joint together limit its movement to prevent dislocation.

Your thighs each have one long bone, called the femur. These are the biggest, strongest bones in your body, and support your full weight. In most adults, these bones are about one quarter of the person's full height. The femurs are linked to your lower legs at the knee joints. These are hinge joints, that only allow you to move your lower legs in an up-and-down direction. At the front of each knee joint is a small bone called the kneecap, or patella, which protects the joint.

Each lower leg has two bones, called the tibia and the fibula. Strong fibres connect these bones to each other. The tibia is much stronger than the fibula and is connected to the lower end of the thigh bone and to the ankle. The weaker fibula is linked to the top of the tibia and to the ankle.

Your lower leg bones end at your ankles. These joints

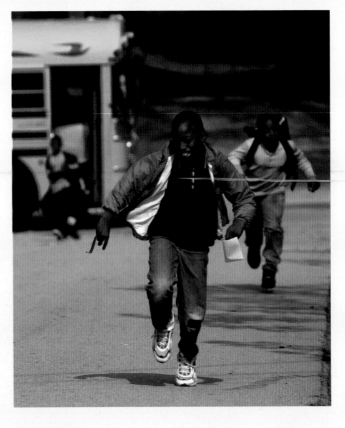

Strong thigh bones carry the full weight of your body when your run.

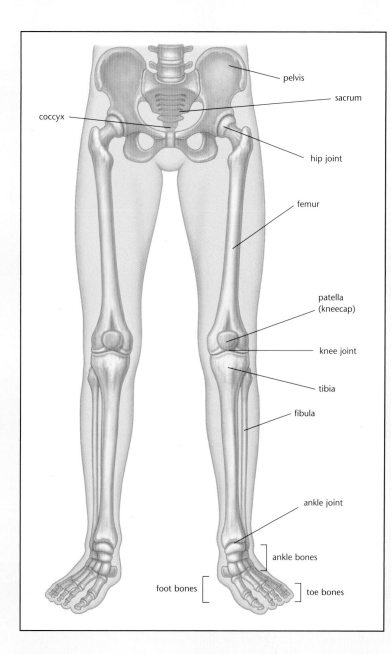

pelvis

sacrum

coccyx

hip joint

femur

patella
(kneecap)

knee joint

tibia

fibula

ankle joint

ankle bones

foot bones

toe bones

In this diagram, you can see how the bones in your legs are arranged.

Case notes

How do doctors replace hips?

Bones can become weak and joints can become damaged and painful as people get older. If a hip joint is damaged, doctors may decide to replace it with an artificial one. The ball of the thigh bone and the socket of the hip bone are removed. A metal joint is inserted in their place. A metal shaft holds the joint into the thigh bone, and a metal or plastic cup is screwed into the hip bone. The new joint allows the person to move his or her hips easily again.

each contain seven bones, which carry the full weight of your body.

The long central part of each foot has five long bones, one leading from the ankle to each toe. Each big toe has two long bones and the other toes each have three long bones. Just as in your hands, the joints between the toe bones are hinge joints, allowing you to bend your toes up and down. The toes are very important in helping you to balance. They are much shorter than your fingers, and cannot make such precise movements.

What are Muscles?

When you think about muscles, you probably think about the ones that help you to move your body. These are called skeletal muscles, and you can control them – for example, you can choose how high to lift a foot, when to nod or shake your head, and which fingers to use to play a piano. Muscles that you can control are called voluntary muscles. These muscles make up more than one third of an adult's body weight.

Skeletal muscle is made up from long thin strands called fibres. These are bound into bundles, which are held together by an outer layer. Blood vessels run in between the bundles of fibres, bringing oxygen and nutrients that the muscle needs, and carrying away waste chemicals made by the muscle. Nerves are also attached to muscle fibres. These carry messages between the brain and the muscle.

Muscles are made up from bundles of fibres.

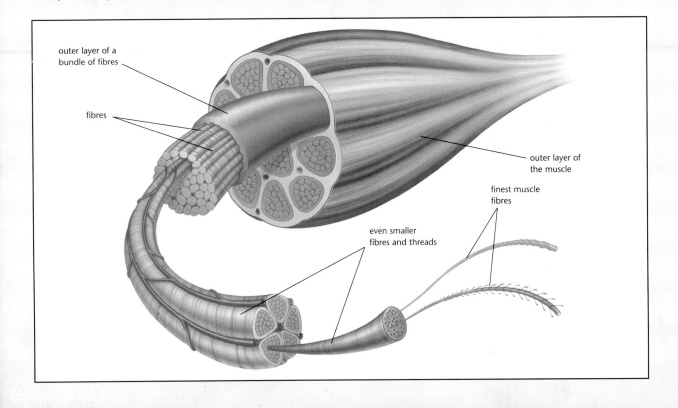

outer layer of a bundle of fibres

fibres

even smaller fibres and threads

outer layer of the muscle

finest muscle fibres

This man is flexing his biceps muscle. If you put one hand on your upper arm and make a fist with your other hand, you should feel your biceps move when you lift your fist!

To move part of your body, your brain sends a signal to a skeletal muscle telling it to contract. To do this, tiny threads inside the muscle fibres slide past each other, making the whole muscle shorter and fatter. To understand how this works, imagine several pencils laid end to end in a long, thin line – if you slide them along so that all the ends are together, you end up with a shorter, fatter bundle.

Most skeletal muscles are attached to bones by tendons. These are strong cords, attached at one end to the muscle and at the other end to the bone. The thickest tendon in your body is the Achilles tendon, which attaches your calf muscle to your heel bone.

There are other important types of muscle as well, which you cannot control. One is cardiac muscle, which your heart is made of. This is very strong muscle and operates continuously throughout your life. Smooth muscle is another type of muscle you cannot control. This forms part of the walls of your digestive organs and helps food to move along your digestive system. Artery walls also contain smooth muscle to help control blood flow.

Case notes

What happens when I get cramp?

Most people will have felt the sharp, stabbing pain of cramp at some time. It happens when a muscle contracts tightly and does not relax. There are several different causes of cramp, including a lack of salt, dehydration and poor blood flow. Sometimes, though, cramp just seems to happen for no reason at all. Gently rubbing the muscle and slowly moving the affected part of your body can help to ease cramp.

Different Muscles

Skeletal muscles come in a variety of different shapes and sizes, depending on the job they have to do. Some are tiny and make very small, precise movements. Others are strong and powerful and are able to make large movements. Muscles can be put into groups according to their shape.

The simplest muscles are thin and not very strong. Bundles of muscle fibres run along the length of the muscle. A muscle like this moves the hyoid bone in your throat when you talk and swallow. Some muscles in your abdomen are also like this.

Some muscles are fat in the middle, with a strong tendon at each end to attach the muscle to neighbouring bones. Again, bundles of muscle fibres run along the length of the muscle. The biceps muscle in your upper arm is like this. It contracts to lift your lower arm.

Some muscles have shorter bundles of fibres, which fan out from a central tendon. These muscles can be very strong. The bundles of fibres can be arranged in a straight line, in a triangular shape, or they can be spread out into a fan shape. Straight muscles allow you to move fingers and toes. The muscles around your

Muscles come in a range of sizes and shapes.

A simple muscle moves the hyoid bone in your throat.

The biceps is attached to a bone at each end.

Straight muscles move your fingers and toes.

Strong, fan-shaped muscles are attached to your shoulder blades.

Rings of muscle move your mouth.

Muscles in your face allow you to smile or frown.

shoulder blades are powerful, fan-shaped muscles. Across your chest, strong triangular muscles are attached to your collarbones, breastbone, ribs and upper arm bone.

Skeletal muscles are not only attached to bone. Your face has more than thirty muscles, attached to skin as well as bone. They contract to allow you to frown, smile and pull your face into all sorts of strange expressions.

In some parts of your body, muscles are arranged in rings. These control the size of openings. Rings of muscle control the shapes of your lips and the iris of your eye. They also control openings from your bladder and digestive system so that you can control when you get rid of body waste.

Case notes

Why are some people paralysed?

When you want to move, signals travel along nerves from your brain to your muscles. These signals make the muscles contract and move your body. If there is a problem with the nerves, the signals cannot reach the muscles, so the muscles do not contract – and the body does not move. This is paralysis and a person suffering from it is said to be paralysed. Paralysis is often the result of an accident in which the spinal cord is damaged.

Pulling Bones

Bones are moved by muscles. When you decide to move a bone, one or more muscles attached to it contract (get shorter). This pulls the bone into a new position. Muscles can only pull bones, they cannot push them. To move a bone back again it has to be pulled by another muscle. For this reason, muscles work in pairs, with each muscle in the pair having an opposite effect to the other.

You can see how a pair of muscles work if you think about raising and lowering your lower arm. To raise your lower arm, your biceps muscle at the front of your upper arm contracts, pulling the bone upwards. This stretches the triceps muscle at the back of your upper arm. To lower your arm again, the triceps muscle contracts, pulling the bone downwards. This stretches the biceps muscle.

Other pairs of muscles all over your body work like this, with one muscle contracting to move a bone in one direction, and another contracting to move it the opposite way. For example, to bend a finger, a muscle in the palm of your hand contracts and pulls the finger bones inwards. To straighten the finger, a muscle on the back of your hand contracts and pulls the bones outwards.

Here you can see how a pair of muscles work in opposite ways to raise and lower your lower arm.

biceps contracts,
lower arm raised

triceps contracts,
lower arm lowers

This toddler is learning to co-ordinate muscle movements in order to walk.

Many of our movements are more complicated than this and involve more pairs of muscles moving several bones in more than one direction. Even a simple step forward is made up of a complex sequence of muscle movements. Many muscles pull on bones in your back and legs, helping you to keep your balance and stay upright.

To be able to make precisely the movement you want takes practice – your brain has to send signals to coordinate all the muscles to move in the right order and at the right time.

Case notes

Fast or slow?

Your skeletal muscles contain two different types of fibre: white fibres and red fibres. These are good at different things. White fibres do not have a good blood supply. They use up their supply of energy very quickly and waste products build up, so they soon become tired. White fibres can contract very quickly for short periods, so they are important for short, fast activities such as sprinting. Red fibres have a good blood supply that brings energy and oxygen and carries away waste products, so they do not become tired quickly. Red fibres contract more slowly but can keep going for a long time, so they are important for activities that last longer, such as cross-country and marathon running.

Looking after Bones and Muscles

Your bones and muscles are very important, so it makes good sense to look after them well. There are some simple things that you can do to make sure your bones and muscles are strong and safe.

Your body uses the food you eat as the raw material for building bones and muscles. A balanced diet, containing plenty of fresh fruit and vegetables, and protein foods such as meat, fish, eggs and nuts, will provide all the essential building blocks your body needs. Starchy foods, such as wholemeal bread, pasta and rice provide plenty of energy for muscles to work. You lose water when you sweat, so it is important to drink plenty, especially in hot weather and when you exercise.

Exercise helps muscles and bones become stronger, so the more you exercise the fitter and healthier your body will be. It is a good idea to try to do some exercise every day – swimming, dancing, cycling and team games are all really good for your muscles and bones.

Some sporting activities can involve some risks. It makes sense to reduce these risks as much as you can, and one way of doing this is to wear the

A balanced diet helps to build strong bones and muscles.

correct protective clothing for your sport. Horse riders wear helmets and often body protectors too. Skateboarders often wear protective pads on elbows and knees. Cyclists should always wear a protective helmet when riding their bikes.

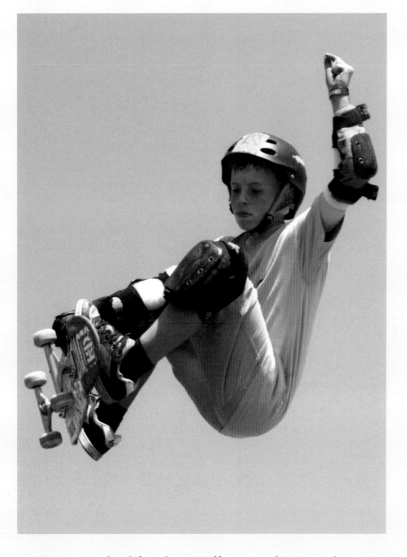

Wearing the right protective clothing for sporting activities can help to prevent accidents and injuries.

Your everyday lifestyle can affect your bones and muscles. Sitting up straight is much better for the muscles and bones of your back than slouching lazily on a sofa. Carrying a rucksack in the middle of your back spreads the weight evenly over your shoulders, rather than having a heavy weight on just one side. Bending at the knees to lift a heavy weight puts less strain on your back than just bending from the waist.

Case notes

Why do I need to warm up before I exercise?

Warming up prepares your bones and muscles for exercise. The fluid inside your joints is gel-like when it is cold, and becomes runnier when it is warmer. You are less likely to damage a warm joint than a cold one, so gentle stretching and flexing of muscles before exercise helps to avoid injury. A few gentle stretches after your exercise is a good idea too, to help you avoid feeling stiff and achy later.

Glossary

bladder — The organ that stores urine.

blood vessel — One of the tubes through which blood travels around the body.

bone marrow — A jelly-like substance inside bones.

brain — The organ that controls every part of the body.

cardiac — To do with the heart.

cartilage — A rubbery material that protects bones.

compact bone — A hard layer of a bone.

contract — Get shorter.

cramp — An unwanted muscle contraction.

digestive system — The organs that break down and absorb food.

fibre — A thin strand.

fuse — Join together.

heart — The organ that pumps blood around the body.

iris — The coloured part of the eye.

joint — The place where two or more bones meet.

ligament — A strong band that holds joints together.

lungs — Organs that are used in breathing.

mineral — A chemical that we need in tiny amounts to maintain health.

nerves — Parts of the body that carry signals to and from the brain.

nutrients — The parts of the food that our bodies can use.

oxygen — A gas that is needed by every part of the body.

skeletal — To do with the skeleton.

spinal cord — The bundle of nerves inside the spinal column.

spongy bone — The inside layer of a bone.

sprain — An injury to a joint.

suture — A join between two skull bones.

synovial membrane — The layer that produces a lubricating fluid at a joint.

tendon — A strong cord that attaches muscles to bones.

Further Information

Books

DK Guide to the Human Body
(Dorling Kindersley, 2004)

Look at Your Body: Muscles by Steve Parker
(Franklin Watts, 1997)

My Healthy Body: Muscles by Jen Green
(Franklin Watts, 2003)

My Healthy Body: Skeleton by Jen Green
(Franklin Watts, 2003)

*The Oxford Children's A to Z of the Human
Body* by Bridget and Neil Ardley (Oxford

Under the Microscope: Muscles
by Clive Gregory (Franklin Watts, 2001)
University Press, 2003)

Under the Microscope: Skeleton by J. Johnson
(Franklin Watts, 2001)

*Usborne Internet-Linked Complete Book of
the Human Body* by Anna Claybourne
(Usborne Publishing, 2003)

Websites

www.kidshealth.org/kid/body/muscles

www.bbc.co.uk/health/kids/bones

www.innerbody.com
click on logo to enter, click on skull picture

Index